FIRST PEOPLES

THE HMONG

OF SOUTHEAST ASIA

SANDRA MILLETT

Lerner Publications Company • Minneapolis

**First American edition published in 2002
by Lerner Publications Company**

Published by arrangement with Times Editions
Copyright © 2002 by Times Media Private Limited

Lerner Publications Company
A division of Lerner Publishing Group
241 First Avenue North
Minneapolis, MN 55401 U.S.A.
Website address: www.lernerbooks.com

Series originated and designed by
Times Editions
An imprint of Times Media Private Limited
A member of the Times Publishing Group
1 New Industrial Road, Singapore 536196
Website address: www.timesone.com.sg/te

Series editors: Margaret J. Goldstein, Paul A. Rozario
Series designers: Tuck Loong, Loo Chuan Ming
Series picture researcher: Susan Jane Manuel

Library of Congress Cataloging-in-Publication Data
Millett, Sandra.
The Hmong of Southeast Asia / by Sandra Millett.
p. cm. — (First peoples)
Includes bibliographical references and index.
ISBN 0-8225-4852-6 (lib. bdg. : alk. paper)
1. Hmong (Asian people)—Juvenile literature. [1. Hmong (Asian people).]
I. Title. II. Series.
DS509.5.H66 M56   2001
305.895'942—dc21   00-012500

Printed in Singapore
Bound in the United States of America

1 2 3 4 5 6—OS—07 06 05 04 03 02

CONTENTS

WHO ARE THE HMONG?

The Hmong are a people of Southeast Asia. Their ancestors were one of the earliest Asian peoples. The Hmong are known by several names: Miao, meaning "young plant" or "sons of the soil"; Meo, the Chinese slang term for cat, a name considered offensive; and Hmong, which is what the people call themselves.

Some people believe that the Hmong originated in Mongolia, a country north of China. The Hmong migrated (traveled) south to eastern China about two thousand years ago.

In Southeast Asia, the Hmong are found in Vietnam, Myanmar (Burma), Laos, and Thailand. Three million Hmong people still live in China, while about 558,000 live in Vietnam. The exact numbers of Hmong in Thailand and Laos aren't known. The Hmong in Southeast Asia generally speak the same language and have the same religious beliefs. But they vary in their customs and traditions.

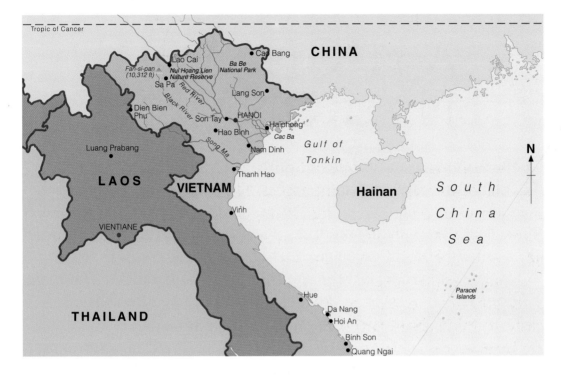

Clans and Distinctive Dress

The Hmong are divided into clans, or subgroups. Each clan wears special clothing with unique stitchery, or embroidery. The major Hmong clans in Vietnam are the White Hmong, Blue Hmong, Black Hmong, and Flower Hmong. The Green Hmong and Armband Hmong, who wear bands on their jacket sleeves, live in Thailand and Laos. The clan names reflect the main color or pattern of the women's clothing. For example, women of the Black Hmong wear black clothing embroidered with cross-stitch designs (made with X-shaped stitches) around the cuffs and collar. Women of the Blue Hmong wear a black and blue costume with a colorful skirt. Flower Hmong women wear elaborate clothes that look like lush bouquets of colorful flowers.

ALL OVER THE WORLD

Many Hmong people live outside Southeast Asia, mainly in the United States. Hmong communities are also located in Argentina, Australia, Canada, France, and French Guiana in South America. The Hmong in these places have adapted to life in their new home countries while still preserving their language and some of the customs of their ancient homelands.

A HIGHLAND ENVIRONMENT

The lush green mountains of northern Vietnam are home to Vietnam's Hmong people. In early summer, the countryside is a quilt of many colors and textures. Sharp mountain peaks rise above dark green plants and trees. Fields of brown earth, glistening wet rice fields, bright green cornfields, and houses with thatched roofs dot the mountainsides and valleys. The main river in northern Vietnam is the Red River, which runs south from China. Small streams drain into the river, which eventually flows past the city of Hanoi and empties into the Gulf of Tonkin in the South China Sea.

Above: Northern Vietnam is home to many species of flowers, including the mountain orchid.

The Elfin Forest

High in the mountains, the soil is poor and the air is cold. This mist-covered region is nicknamed the elfin forest because the plants growing here are stunted. Gnarled trees cling to the steep mountain faces, along with lichens and flowering plants such as orchids. Hmong boys sometimes go into the high country with their fathers to gather firewood and wild plants to be used as medicines and in religious ceremonies. But climbing here is very hard because of the low levels of oxygen in the air. Thick clouds coat the slopes like cotton fluff, creating an eerie atmosphere.

A High Peak

At 10,312 feet (3,140 meters) above sea level, Fan-si-pan is Vietnam's highest mountain. Dwarf bamboo plants, small shrubs, and rhododendrons grow along its ridge. Plants on the exposed western slope of Fan-si-pan grow close to the ground for protection from the wind and cold. No one lives on Fan-si-pan because of the high altitude (distance above sea level), harsh terrain, and winter snow.

Above: Farmers grow rice in terraces in the Sa Pa valley of northern Vietnam.

The Town of Sa Pa

Many Hmong live in and around the town of Sa Pa in northern Vietnam. It lies high in the mountains near the Nui Hoang Lien Nature Reserve. The average temperature in Sa Pa is 60 degrees Fahrenheit (15.6 degrees Celsius). In summer, temperatures can be as high as 85 degrees Fahrenheit (29.4 degrees Celsius). The coolest period is December to February, when snow falls.

Below: Mist rises on the slopes of mountains near the town of Sa Pa.

MONSOON SEASON

The monsoon season, from May to September, brings heavy rainfall to Southeast Asia. The water cascades down the mountainsides (*above*). It floods rivers and streams, washes away soil, and turns the rivers brown with mud. The rain also turns paths muddy and slippery and makes walking dangerous. The Hmong are used to walking in this terrain. Visitors, however, sometimes need to use walking sticks for support on the muddy paths.

PLANTING IN THE HIGHLANDS

The Nui Hoang Lien Nature Reserve is a forested area in northwestern Vietnam. The mountains here are formed of granite. Over time, the rock has worn away, leaving behind a clay soil called china clay. Very slippery when wet, this clay is used to make porcelain and china dishes. There are no Hmong villages in the reserve, but six villages are scattered across the nearby mountains and valleys.

Above: Harvesting rice is hard work.

Right: Muddy rice terraces line the mountainsides of northern Vietnam.

Planting on Slopes

The flat land in the valleys of northern Vietnam can't grow enough food for everyone, so Hmong farmers plant rice and corn on terraces along the slopes of many mountains. To build the terraces, farmers cut away parts of the mountainside to make flat areas for planting. They build walls around the fields to keep the soil in place. Some terrace walls are 10 feet (3 meters) high.

Thinning Mountain Forests

Above: Much of the forests of northern Laos has been cleared to create fields for farming.

At one time, the mountains of northern Vietnam were covered with dense forests. After more than two hundred years of human settlement, the area is still green. But much of the original forest is gone. People cut down many of the forests on the steep slopes and planted crops on the cleared land. They used the trees for firewood and to build houses.

To repair damage to the environment, the Vietnamese government has organized tree-planting programs in the Sa Pa region. The new trees will help cover the soil once again and will help preserve the land for future generations.

FIELDS AND FORESTS

Trails wind along the hillsides, connecting the fields to the small villages of the Hmong and other groups. If a field is not planted, grasses, bushes, and small trees will quickly grow there. Water buffalo will graze on the small plants and grasses. Higher up in the mountains, the forests remain much as they always have been. There are no fields or roads at this altitude. The only way to travel here is to hike through dense growth up the steep mountainsides.

HIGHLAND WILDLIFE

In the past, the Hmong hunted red deer, wild boars, foxes, and tigers. Because of hunting, and because the forests where the animals normally live have been cleared, many species have become endangered. To protect the remaining wildlife, the Vietnamese government has outlawed hunting and the sale of stuffed wild animals.

Above: The stump-tailed macaque is an endangered animal.

Above: A forest squirrel

Forest Giants

About sixty kinds of mammals live in the Nui Hoang Lien Nature Reserve. Tigers were once common here but are now rare. The Asiatic black bear and the stump-tailed macaque have become rare as well. Usually, visitors to the reserve see only small mammals, such as squirrels and other rodents.

Endangered!

Because of illegal hunting and the destruction of forests to create farmland, seventeen of the animal species that live in the Nui Hoang Lien Nature Reserve are rare or endangered. These animals include the tiger, the clouded leopard, the black gibbon, and the binturong, a small animal related to the cat. The Vietnamese government and concerned citizens are taking steps to protect the wildlife. In Ba Be National Park in Cao Bang province, for example, many groups, including the Hmong, are working with conservation programs funded by the United Nations, an international organization.

Above: The forests of northern Vietnam are home to many varieties of tropical birds, including the colorful parrot.

A DIVERSE ECOSYSTEM

Vietnam has always had one of the most diverse animal populations in the world. In the 1920s, French-American biologist Jean Theodore Delacour visited northern Vietnam many times and discovered new kinds of birds. In 1929, Theodore Jr. and Kermit Roosevelt, sons of U.S. President Theodore Roosevelt, led an expedition to Vietnam and collected many species of mammals, including tigers (*above*). The animals collected by Delacour and the Roosevelt brothers can still be seen at the Field Museum in Chicago, Illinois. Collecting wild animals is no longer legal, however.

ANCIENT FARMERS

Chinese historical documents mention the Hmong as early as 2700 B.C. For centuries, the Hmong were farmers. Every ten years or so, as the soil became less fertile from farming, the people moved on to another mountain and began clearing the land once more. Men taught their sons how to plant crops, harvest, and hunt animals for food. They taught them the importance of clan unity (togetherness) and leadership. Women taught their daughters how to cook, make clothes decorated with elaborate stitchery, work in the fields alongside the men, and take care of the home and children.

Slash-and-Burn

In earlier times, the Hmong practiced slash-and-burn agriculture. High on the mountainsides in January, men and boys would prepare an area for rice planting. They used axes and knives to cut down trees and clear fields. In late March or early April, they burned the dried brush and trees. The ash produced by the fires made the soil more fertile. But, over the years, this practice also destroyed much of the forest and polluted the air. For this reason, slash-and-burn farming is no longer allowed in Vietnam.

Right: The Hmong still harvest rice using ancient methods.

The Planting and Growing Season

In May, Hmong women and children dug weeds and turned the soil over with sticks. They poked holes in the ground and dropped rice grains in each hole. The rice crop was harvested in October or November.

Above: A piece of decorated fabric called a story cloth shows the ancient, traditional Hmong way of life. These decorated fabrics are also called *paj ntaub*, or stitchery.

The Harvest

Once the rice stalks were harvested, the farmers dried and threshed, or beat, the stalks, releasing the grains. They spread the grains on straw mats to dry in the sun. Next, using large shallow baskets, women and girls threw the rice into the air. The wind would blow away the dirt, and the rice would fall back onto clean mats. Using a bowl called a mortar and a stone called a pestle, the farmers then pounded the rice to remove the husks. Finally, the rice was ready for storage and cooking.

ANCIENT HERO

King Chi You is an ancient hero for the Hmong of southern China. He was a Hmong leader who lived in southern China about 5,000 years ago. He united many different tribes under his rule. The Chinese also consider him one of the important kings of ancient China. The life of King Chi You is now part of Hmong folktales.

OUT OF CHINA

I n China, the Hmong were treated harshly by the Chinese, who called them "barbarians." From the 1600s to the 1900s, Chinese rulers taxed the Hmong heavily and forced them to perform corvée—to work on road building and other government projects without pay.

Above: The French built many big villas in Sa Pa in northern Vietnam.

Moving South

In the late 1700s and early 1800s, some Hmong fled southern China. At first, about eighty Hmong families entered northern Vietnam. The largest movement of Hmong people into Vietnam occurred after 1868, when more than 10,000 Hmong fled south after an unsuccessful revolt.

Contact with Outsiders

The Hmong first came into contact with Europeans when the French gained control of Vietnam, ruling from 1859 to 1954. A French missionary, or religious teacher, arrived in Sa Pa in 1918. More French colonists (settlers) followed. They liked Sa Pa's climate and scenery. In 1932, they began turning the region into a vacation spot. The French moved the Black Hmong settlements away from Sa Pa to gain land for construction. They built many buildings, as well as a large church, tennis courts, and a power station.

Right: Hmong living in Thailand in the 1890s pose for the camera.

Under French Rule

Life for the Hmong was no better under French control than it had been under the Chinese. Beginning in the early 1900s, the Hmong and other minority groups revolted against the French. From 1919 to 1921 a revolt known as the Madman's War raged over northern Indochina. Once again, taxes and corvée were at the heart of the conflicts between the Hmong people and their rulers. Revolts against the French failed, however. Because of the revolts, the Hmong earned a reputation for being aggressive and warlike.

Above: A modern Hmong story cloth shows the Hmong moving south from China.

INDOCHINA

French traders and missionaries arrived in Southeast Asia in the 1500s and 1600s. But it was not until the mid-1800s that they began to take control of parts of Southeast Asia. Between 1858 and 1893, France conquered Vietnam, Laos, and Cambodia. The French ruled these three countries as a single region. They called this region Indochina.

15

DIVIDED BY WAR

In August 1945, Ho Chi Minh declared that Vietnam was an independent country. He named it the Democratic Republic of Vietnam and became its first president. The French tried to retake control of Vietnam, sparking off the First Indochina War (1946–1954). At the end of the war, Vietnam was divided into communist North Vietnam and non-communist South Vietnam.

Below: The U.S. Army trained Hmong soldiers in Laos during the Second Indochina War.

The Vietnam War

Between 1957 and 1975, during the Second Indochina War, the communists in the north struggled for control of all of Vietnam. To support South Vietnam's independence and to fight communism, the United States officially entered into the conflict in 1965. Fifty-eight thousand Americans and almost two million Vietnamese were killed in what became known as the Vietnam War.

The Hmong Join the War

The conflict crossed into Laos in the early 1960s. At this time, some Hmong groups agreed to join the U.S. Army Special Forces, known as the Green Berets, to fight in a secret army. The U.S. Central Intelligence Agency (CIA) promised that the United States would find new homes for the Hmong fighters if they lost the war.

Above: A town burns in North Vietnam during the Vietnam War.

The Defeat of South Vietnam

The communists won control of South Vietnam in 1975. North and South Vietnam were then reunified as the Socialist Republic of Vietnam. Hanoi became the capital. The country continued to suffer. Many people in the south resisted the new communist laws. Many South Vietnamese became refugees, fleeing the country on foot and by boat.

Taking Sides

Depending on where they lived, the Hmong fought on opposite sides in the Vietnam War. The Vietnamese Hmong sided with the communists and remained in Vietnam after reunification. Some Hmong in Laos fought with the Americans against the communists. These fighters had two choices after the war ended. They could either escape to refugee camps in Thailand or face death at the hands of the communists.

HO CHI MINH

Ho Chi Minh (1890–1969), whose real name was Nguyen Tat Thanh, was born in Vietnam. Ho (*right*) went to school in Hue, the country's ancient capital. He traveled to Paris and tried to convince the French government to grant Vietnam's independence. But he was unsuccessful. He then began to read about communism. The communists wanted to end private ownership and to distribute wealth to everyone equally. Ho returned to Vietnam in 1925. Five years later, he became leader of the Indochinese Communist Party, which fought for independence for Vietnam.

NEW HOMELANDS

With the help of foreign governments, many Laotian Hmong found safe, new homes in Australia, France, and other countries after the war. The largest number of Hmong refugees moved to the United States, especially to Rhode Island, Wisconsin, Minnesota, Kansas, Colorado, Washington, and California.

Above: A group of Hmong at a picnic in St. Paul, Minnesota

Feeling Lost

Overnight, the Hmong left behind their traditional lifestyle and moved into the computer age. Most could not speak, read, or write English. They did not know how to drive, read road signs, or use appliances that people in the United States take for granted. With no money to buy land and little knowledge of modern farming, many of the Hmong had to accept welfare.

Left: Hmong children in St. Paul, Minnesota, play at a drinking fountain.

The Hmong in California

Once in the United States, many Hmong moved a second time to be near family members in Fresno, a city in central California. Fresno soon had a population of 58,000 Hmong, the largest Hmong community in the United States. Fresno's government and schools struggled to make changes to help the Hmong, who did not speak English or know anything about U.S. culture.

Adapting to New Lives

Some people in Fresno objected to the Hmong newcomers. But most people realized that the Hmong were in the United States because they had supported and fought with U.S. soldiers during the Vietnam War. Concerned U.S. citizens formed groups to help the new residents. The Hmong also formed support groups to help one another. They took language classes and learned how to live in a new culture.

Young Hmong people soon began attending college. Many Hmong men took classes in computers and medicine. Many women studied law, medicine, and education.

Right: An American Hmong boy reads a book.

A STRANGER IN A STRANGE LAND

Imagine you are a seventeen-year-old boy who has fought alongside American soldiers in the secret war in Laos. After escaping over the mountains and living in a refugee camp, you and your family finally resettle in Fresno, California. You speak no English and are used to farming and to fighting a war. Now you have to attend high school in a strange country. Would you feel out of place? Would it be hard to adjust?

AN AGRICULTURAL ECONOMY

The Hmong in Southeast Asia continue to live mainly as farmers. They plant, tend, and harvest rice on terraces built into the mountain slopes. Rice grows best in flooded fields, so the farmers flood the terraces with water. They work in mud and water up to their thighs and plunge rice seedlings into the mud with their hands.

Making a Living

Because of the high altitude, the growing season in Sa Pa is short, and rice is harvested once a year. Many families can't grow enough rice to last year-round. The Vietnamese government provides extra rice to the poorest families.

Hmong Crops

The main Hmong food crops are rice for the people and corn for the animals. Cash crops—those that are sold instead of eaten on the farm—include sugarcane, manioc (a plant with edible roots), peanuts, green beans, cucumbers, and squash.

Left: Corn is an important crop in northern Vietnam. The Hmong grow corn for animal feed.

Everyone Helps Out

Everyone in a Hmong family works. Both men and women labor in the fields and do heavy physical work. In the fields, men usually prepare the soil for planting with handmade wooden plows pulled by water buffalo. The elderly who can no longer work in the fields look after the children at home. Women and girls do the housework and most of the child care. Women and children care for the animals.

Above: A Hmong couple in the Sa Pa valley work their flooded rice terrace with a water buffalo.

Useful Animals

Animals are important to the Hmong. Each Hmong family raises chickens, potbellied pigs, goats, and cattle, which are killed for meat. Some families also own horses, which carry grain to and from the fields. Water buffalo pull plows.

Left: Women in northern Vietnam plunge rice seedlings into the soft mud.

CHILDREN'S DUTIES

A Hmong girl (*right*) must get up before her parents and begin the day's housework. In her free time, she must make paj ntaub. Boys herd goats on grassy hillsides or ride on the backs of water buffalo to the family fields. They learn from their fathers how to make the water buffalo plow the fields. Children also tend the water buffalo, weed fields, harvest crops, and help with other lighter farmwork and household duties.

ECONOMIC CHANGES IN VIETNAM

The Hmong are the eighth largest minority group in Vietnam, numbering 558,000. They have leaders in government but their living conditions remain poor. In Sa Pa, the poorest clans struggle to provide food, clothing, and housing for their families. Few Hmong children attend school regularly.

Above: Children in a Hmong village in northern Laos

Health and Health Care

In some Hmong villages, children suffer from a poor diet or from lack of food. Modern health care is available, but people often have to walk long distances to reach medical clinics. Many clans rely on a medicine man for healing since modern medicines are either not available or are too expensive.

Slash-and-Burn Farming

Above: Farmers in northern Thailand still clear land for farming using the slash-and-burn method.

Vietnam's ban on slash-and-burn farming has hurt the Hmong. Because the farmers can no longer clear the forests high on the mountains, they have less land for growing crops. Some clans have moved to villages in valleys along rivers and next to roads. The Hmong use traditional farming practices on these lands, with no modern equipment or farming techniques. Because they lack good land and equipment, Hmong farms are not successful.

A Banned Crop

The Hmong made opium from opium poppies long before they left China. Opium poppies were easy to grow. They could be harvested the first year of planting. Their harvest time did not interrupt the harvesting of other crops. The plant did not harm the soil. In 1954, Vietnam banned commercial opium poppy farming, although people could still grow and make opium for personal use. Using opium leads to addiction and other health problems, so the Vietnamese government outlawed all opium poppy farming in 1986.

Left: The Hmong in Laos grow pineapples as a cash crop.

NEW CROPS

Vietnam outlawed opium poppy farming in the 1980s. The Hmong in Vietnam looked for other crops to raise to earn money. They began growing an herb called ginseng and a plant called ginger. Ginseng is an important ingredient in traditional Chinese medicines. Ginger is also used in Chinese medicines and is a common ingredient in Chinese cooking.

A NEW MEANS OF LIVELIHOOD

The Hmong are developing new ways to earn money. These new sources of income include tourism and selling unique Hmong clothing. Hmong women and girls do much of the work in both businesses.

Below: A Hmong girl sells stitchery in a Laotian street market.

The Growth of Tourism

Vietnam is attracting more and more tourists from all over the world. Tourists visit the area to enjoy the beautiful scenery, the warm climate, and the culture of the hill peoples, including the Hmong. New hotels greet the growing numbers of visitors. Tour operators offer visitors the chance to trek through parts of northern Vietnam. Popular sights for visitors are Dien Bien Phu, a town on the border with Laos, and Fan-si-pan, Vietnam's highest peak.

Above: A Black Hmong girl in Sa Pa guides American tourists.

Above: Women sell fresh produce at Sa Pa's weekly market.

Making Friends and Selling Stitchery

Groups of young Black Hmong girls greet visitors as they arrive in Sa Pa. The girls introduce themselves to the visitors and tie colorful handwoven string bracelets around their wrists as a sign of friendship and good luck. Many of the girls speak some simple English, learned from English-speaking tourists. From Sa Pa, the Hmong guides take the visitors to villages in the mountains. There, the Hmong sell their stitchery and jewelry to the visitors.

Changing Lives

Hmong families earn money from jobs in tourism. But these new jobs also pull young people away from traditional ways of life. In southern China, for example, many young Hmong people take jobs working with tourists instead of farming as their parents and ancestors did.

SA PA'S COLORFUL MARKET

Saturday is market day in Sa Pa. Many hill people, including the Hmong, come to the town. Produce in the market (*below*) is displayed in open-air stalls. You can find skinned cow heads and pig organs. Some merchants sell bamboo shoots and other vegetables. Shoes, baskets, garments, and jewelry are also on sale at the colorful market.

TRADITIONAL HOMES

The Hmong build their homes out of wood and bamboo. The walls of the houses are made from wood or bamboo pieces tied together. There are spaces between the pieces. In the winter, it gets very cold inside the house as wind blows through the cracks.

The Hmong also use bamboo to make bridges, fences, and other structures. The roofs of Hmong houses are made of thatch—thick mats of straw.

Above: Hmong children in northern Thailand take a nap on the bamboo floor of their school.

Simple Interiors

Hmong houses have no running water or plumbing. The children haul water in bamboo buckets from the closest river or stream. The home fire is built directly on the hard dirt floor in the center of the house, sometimes surrounded by a barrier made of sticks. Hmong houses don't have chimneys—smoke escapes directly through the thatched roofs. Family members share raised sleeping platforms, covered with thin straw mats, that line one wall of the house.

Right: Black pigs wander in the yard of a Hmong house in northern Thailand.

Preparing a Meal

Hmong people cook indoors over an open fire. A typical Hmong meal consists of rice, vegetables, and perhaps some meat. Corn for the animals is first crushed in a large, hinged wooden machine that sits in the corner of the house. The crushed kernels are then boiled and fed to the animals.

Above: A Hmong family in northern Thailand prepares a meal in their home.

In the Yard

Some families raise livestock for sale, and all families keep livestock for food. Chickens, potbellied pigs, and goats live outside the house. A bamboo fence surrounding the yard prevents the animals from wandering away. Water buffalo are kept in small thatched huts near the house. To enter the yard, people climb a ladder leaning against the bamboo fence.

NOTES FOR GUESTS

Hmong families hang a piece of red fabric over the entryway of their homes as a sign of welcome. However, visitors must always ask permission from a male member of the family before entering the house. Guests must also take off their shoes before going inside the home and must not step on the doorsill. Inside the home, visitors should pay attention to their movements. For example, don't point your fingers at anyone. And don't cross your legs so that your feet point at someone else. These gestures are considered rude.

VILLAGES AND CLANS

Hmong villages have between 2 and 150 houses. Sometimes single houses are scattered up mountain slopes. But usually houses are clustered together, with people of the same clan living near one another. Each Hmong village has its own territory, chief, and strict rules.

Above: Hmong farmers in northern Thailand share their midday meal.

The Way of the Clans

Over centuries of moving to new lands, Hmong family ties are still strong. Extended families often live and die together in the same house, with as many as four generations living together. Family ties are so strong that Hmong people of the same lineage, or family line, are expected to support and help one another, even if doing so costs them their lives. Those who share the same lineage are called a "cluster of brothers" or "a ceremonial household." Hmong people respect and honor the elderly. The elderly know that their families will take care of them and respect them even if they cannot work.

Above: A Hmong family works in the fields. Families often exchange labor. One day they work in their own fields. The next day, they work in the fields of their clan members.

Strong Bonds Overseas

Hmong who live overseas maintain close ties with those in the same clan and those of the same lineage. But Westerners don't usually live as close to family members as people do in Southeast Asia. This difference can be difficult for Hmong immigrants to the United States. One Hmong mother living in the United States complained that her daughter had married and moved "so far away." In this instance, "far away" was only 1 mile (1.6 kilometers).

Above: An American Hmong family visits their ancestral homeland in Laos.

Continuing the Traditions

"The Hmong way" has been nurtured over the centuries and continues to this day, even in the United States. The Hmong language, duties, and loyalty to the clan are of great importance, as is respect for elders. Whether in Vietnam or the United States, a Hmong person will always ask another Hmong his or her age upon meeting. Age determines how new acquaintances will address one another. Hmong use titles such as Honored Uncle, Younger Brother, or Esteemed Mother.

Below: A cluster of traditional houses in northern Vietnam

CLAN RULES

In general, Hmong clans in Thailand, Laos, and Vietnam share many things in common. But some clans have very specific rules. For example, the Lis and the Yaj clans of Thailand allow members to eat only certain foods. Members of the Haam clan will not take cooked rice with them for lunch in the rice fields. They believe they will turn into snakes if they do.

THE HMONG AND MARRIAGE

Marriage and family are the foundations of Hmong life. Young people marry between the ages of fourteen and eighteen. Marriages are forbidden between men and women of the same lineage. Men are the head of the family. They may practice polygamy, marrying more than one woman.

Preparations for Marriage

Childhood is a time for a Hmong girl to learn how to run a home and to be a wife and mother. She must learn how to clean and cook. When her daily chores are done for the day, she must create elaborate stitchery and clothes to be worn and sold. Being good with a needle and thread is highly valued in the Hmong culture. Boys also work. They learn how to farm so that they can someday support a wife and children and provide for the elders in the family. Boys learn how to choose good farmland and how to act as head of the household.

Above: Learning to sew is an important part of a Hmong girl's education.

Wedding Rituals

Traditionally, fathers planned marriages for their children. Modern Hmong marriages, however, are often arranged without the parents' consent. The marriage might include a mock "kidnapping" of the bride, organized by the groom. The groom must also follow the age-old ritual of paying a bride-price, a sum of money given to the parents of the bride.

The Dutiful Daughter-in-Law

The newly married bride and groom do not live on their own right away. Instead they live with the husband's parents. A Hmong wife hopes that her husband's mother will be good to her. They will live and work together for several years. The couple may not move out until they have two or three children. A good wife has to respect the elderly members of her husband's family. She must give the best food to her father-in-law and the family elders. She must work hard and be kind. The parents show their appreciation by saying that she is a good wife.

Left: A Hmong couple celebrate a courtship ritual in northern Thailand.

MARRIED LIFE

Once a Hmong woman (*right*) marries and enters her husband's home, the family holds a ceremony honoring the memory of the ancestors. The woman no longer has the right to return to her parents' home unless she has permission from her in-laws and is accompanied by her husband. A Hmong husband and wife do not touch in public and do not walk side by side. Usually, the husband walks ahead of his wife. It is also a sign of disrespect to touch or walk in front of an elder.

LANGUAGE AND LEGENDS

The Hmong did not have a written form of their language until the 1900s. The written form of the language was introduced in 1952 by missionaries. The alphabet they came up with is used by Hmong in many parts of the world to communicate with each other.

The Hmong Book

A Hmong legend explains why they did not have a written language until recently. The legend says that, long ago, there was a book written on a piece of cloth. This book was very precious to the Hmong. They carried the book with them when they fled China. Along the way, the book got wet. People stretched it out to dry. But cows began eating the cloth. Little remained by the time they were chased away. The following night, the Hmong discovered that rats had eaten all the remaining pieces of their precious book.

Right: A teacher instructs Hmong students at a school for refugee children in Laos.

Similarities and Differences

All Hmong people speak the same basic language. Some words do vary between Vietnamese and Laotian Hmong people, or even among clans. To communicate with other groups in Vietnam, some Hmong also speak Vietnamese. The Hmong in Laos also use Laotian. Hmong in Thailand also speak the Thai language. Standard Hmong—the version written down in books—is based on the language spoken in the Sa Pa region.

Above: Hmong kids at an outdoor class in northern Vietnam

Above: Hmong girls at a school in Thailand

Changing Tones, Changing Meaning

Hmong is a tonal language. Changing the tone, or pitch, of a word changes its meaning. In Hmong writing, the final letter of a word indicates the tone. The letter *b* signals a high tone, *j* signals a high falling tone, *v* stands for a mid-rising tone, *g* stands for a breathy mid-low tone, *s* signals a low tone, and *m* indicates a creaky low falling tone. For instance, in Hmong writing, paj ntaub is the term for stitchery. The *j* at the end of the first word indicates a high falling tone, and the *b* at the end of the second word indicates a high tone. But the final letters are silent, so paj ntaub is pronounced "pahn-DAH-OH." In English, the term is sometimes also spelled pa 'ndau.

INTO THE INTERNET AGE

The Hmong language has moved into the twenty-first century thanks to computers and the Internet. Many Hmong websites introduce the language to both Hmong and non-Hmong. On-line Hmong-English dictionaries and websites teach the pronunciation of Hmong words and help document the language. These resources are very useful, especially for Hmong who no longer live in Southeast Asia and may not use the Hmong language on a daily basis. The Internet helps them keep up with their language.

COLORFUL CLOTHING

Each Hmong clan has distinctive clothing, and costumes vary greatly among clans. If Hmong people from different clans, villages, or countries gathered together, observers would not even realize that the people belonged to the same overall group. Women in each clan wear elaborate head coverings and skirts. Men generally wear full-length black trousers, a black vest, and a jacket that might be embroidered with cross-stitch.

Below: Colorful and elaborate Hmong festival clothes

Sa Pa Style

In Sa Pa, White Hmong women wear handwoven white skirts. Black Hmong women wear black clothing. Red Hmong women wear red head coverings and indigo (blue) skirts decorated with red fabric. The women of the Flower Hmong wear the most elaborate and colorful skirts and tops, with a scarf for a head wrap.

Right: Indigo (blue) dye is made by boiling the leaves of the indigo plant.

Hemp Clothes

Hmong clothes are made of hemp, a fabric created from the hemp plant. After drying the hemp stalks, women peel off the outer layers and strip them into long fibers. They twist the ends together to make long threads. Once twisted into threads, the hemp is woven into hemp cloth. It is often decorated and dyed indigo. The dyeing can take from ten days to one month. Once dyed, the fabric is made into clothes. Hemp cloth is very sturdy and lasts for a long time.

Left: A Hmong woman strips fiber from a hemp stalk.

The Batik Method

Hmong clothes are sometimes dyed using batik, an ancient method of making a design on fabric with melted wax. The centuries-old technique was developed in Indonesia. Using melted beeswax that flows from a special tool, the artist draws straight or zigzag patterns onto fabric. The waxed fabric is then placed in a bath of dark blue dye, made by boiling the leaves of the indigo plant. Once dyed, the fabric is boiled to remove the wax, exposing the patterns previously covered by wax.

HMONG JEWELRY

Like Hmong clothing, Hmong jewelry (*above*) differs depending on the clan. For example, Black Hmong wear engraved necklaces that open in the front. The necklaces are made of long ropes of small metal rings. The Flower Hmong necklace opens in the back. It is a single chain holding a cluster of tiny bells, animals, and other shapes.

STITCHERY

Hmong do not place importance on items such as furniture or appliances. But their paj ntaub (stitchery) is important from birth to death. A family shows its social position and wealth by wearing fancy hand-stitched clothing.

Above: Elaborate and colorful Hmong stitchery

Exquisite Needlework

Every Hmong mother teaches her daughters paj ntaub. In English the word means "flower cloth." The geometric designs of paj ntaub are used to decorate clothes, burial cloths, belts, purses, hats, and baby carriers. Some designs are named for animals. For example, swirls in Laotian paj ntaub are called "snail houses" because they look like snails' shells. Others designs are named "elephant's foot" and "ram's head." Some designs are cross-stitched—created with tiny X-shaped stitches. Hmong women also cut folded fabric to create appliqués, much like making paper snowflakes. The sewer cuts the fabric with tiny snips. She turns the cut edges under as she sews the appliqué to a background cloth with hundreds of tiny stitches.

Left: A Flower Hmong girl wearing a traditional outfit enjoys a bowl of noodles in Sa Pa market in northern Vietnam.

Above: Hmong festival clothes are especially elaborate and colorful.

Sewing and Hmong Customs

Girls display their skills, creativity, and talent through their stitchery. When a Hmong girl is ready to marry, her value as a wife depends partly on her needlework skills. During courtship, girls spend a lot of time making skirts that they will wear as brides and new wives. They will wear their best clothing to marriage parties and to the New Year celebration of Tet. A Hmong bride-to-be makes elaborate garments to take to her husband's house.

Baby Clothes

Hmong babies and children up to about age ten often wear hats. These round black caps, some with earflaps, are decorated with stitchery, coins, beads, and bright pom-poms and tassels. As with women's clothing, the hat styles vary with different clans.

Right: The colorful cap of a Hmong infant

A MODERN METHOD OF EMBROIDERY

Hmong women use treadle sewing machines (*left*) to make much of their elaborate clothing. This kind of machine does not run on electricity. The user powers it by pushing a flat foot pedal connected to the gears with a leather loop. The faster the peddling, the faster the machine stitches. Using sewing machines, women can make clothing much faster than they can by hand. But even with a machine, a skirt can take a month to complete.

SONGS AND MUSIC

The Hmong people are known for their beautiful songs. Each clan has its own love songs, work songs, and festival songs. Music accompanies courtship, weddings, and funerals. Historically, Hmong songs were passed down orally (by word of mouth) from one generation to the next. The Flower Hmong are especially well known for their beautiful music.

Above: The bamboo flute is a popular musical instrument among Hmong in northern Vietnam.

Traditional Instruments

Hmong musical instruments include the *qeej*, a bamboo wind instrument, the *gó lung jià*, a two-stringed violin, and flutes, gongs, and drums. Hmong musicians also play cymbals, trumpets, and instruments made from water buffalo horns. The *puae* is a trumpet played at village festivals to greet visitors in the morning.

Left: An illustration of a Hmong qeej player in southern China

The Qeej

The qeej is an instrument made from bamboo and wood. It has six long pipes of different lengths, much like a Scottish bagpipe. To produce sounds, the player inhales and exhales through the pipes. The upper and lower pipes produce a drone, or background sound, while the inner pipes play the tune. Only men are allowed to play the qeej. It is used for funerals and festivals, but it can't be used to play love songs.

Love Songs and Poems

Unmarried Hmong teenagers gather in large groups at Sa Pa's Chó Tinh area, called the "love market." Here, the girls sing love songs over and over, and the boys play instruments and sing. Although they do not date, the young people talk and decide whom they will marry. A boy will sing a poem about his feelings to a girl he likes, making up lyrics like this: "There is a tree on the hill. Its flowers are beautiful like the clouds in the sky. Having heard that you are a pretty girl, we come to see you for an engagement." The sung poems are called *kwv txhiaj*.

Left: The qeej is an important instrument for the Hmong.

MUSIC OF THE LEAF

Leaves (*right*) are favorite Hmong instruments. Hmong can play music with a leaf by placing an edge between the lips and blowing. The resulting sound is high pitched, clear, and very lovely.

MYTHS AND SPIRITS

The Hmong believe that the universe is divided into physical and spiritual worlds. Spirits, which must be consulted on all important matters, rule both of these worlds. The Hmong also believe that every person has a life-soul, necessary for happiness and health. Its loss can result in illness. Sorrow, fright, anger, curiosity, or the urge to travel are things that might separate a person from his or her life-soul.

Hmong Creation Story

A Hmong myth says that in the beginning, heaven and earth were joined. Spirits and people lived together in harmony. A frog created this unified world, which was destroyed when people killed the frog. Before dying, the frog separated heaven and earth, so humans could not cross over into the spirit world. Death and sickness filled the land of humans from then on.

Left: This Hmong dancer in China wears a mask that represents a spirit. Other dance masks represent ancient folk heroes.

The Origin of the Shamans

Siv Yis, the first shaman, spent many years curing sick people. At his death, he promised to return to earth and help humankind. Coming down the stairs that connected heaven to earth, Siv Yis realized that humankind was asleep and had not been preparing for his return. Angry, he threw down his magical healing tools. People on earth who found the tools discovered that they could cure the sick. These healers became the next shamans.

Above: The Hmong believe that spirits inhabit natural objects such as waterfalls.

Other Hmong Myths

Xob is the god of thunder. He is a winged animal who was once imprisoned inside a cage. He escaped one day and flew away across the rice fields, making loud booming noises that humans hear as thunder.

WATER DRAGONS

According to Hmong beliefs, water dragons are spirits that live in water. Zaj Laug is the oldest of the dragons and rules the waters that surround the earth. Zaj Laug also controls the rain. Zaj Laug is very important to the Hmong, since heavy rainfall leads to a good harvest and lots of food. The photo above shows a dragon dance.

SPIRITS, BIRTH, AND DEATH

Each spirit, or *dab*, has its own name, personality, and power. The spirit may live in a rock, tree, rice field, animal, or person. If someone falls ill or has an accident, or if the harvest is bad, people believe spirits are responsible. Most villages have their own shaman, who acts as a go-between with the spirit world.

Above: A Hmong infant in Laos

Hmong Births

The Hmong consult the spirit world the third day after a baby is born. On this day, the baby is named in a ceremony called *hu plig*. New babies are small. So the Hmong believe that their souls can be stolen by a dab or lured away by a loud noise or sweet smell. Another birth ritual involves the placenta, the organ that helps nourish a baby in the womb. If a girl is born, the placenta is buried under the bed. A boy's placenta will be buried beneath the main pillar of the house, near the altar to the family's ancestors. The Hmong believe that a dead soul will reclaim its placenta before beginning its journey to the ancestors.

Right: Some Hmong in Southeast Asia have converted to Christianity. Many Hmong in the United States are also Christians.

Above: At the end of a funeral, a gate is erected to invite the spirit of the dead person to be reborn.

Ancestor Worship

The Hmong worship dead ancestors at an altar in the home. In this way, the Hmong honor their dead relatives, whom they respected and obeyed when alive. Hmong ancestor worship creates a bond between the living and the dead—and among the past, present, and future.

Hmong Funerals

When a Hmong person dies, the family calls for the *nong rua*, the man responsible for spiritual matters. He washes the body and dresses it in formal clothes. The body is then laid near the house's spiritual pole, the main support pillar. Later, the body is taken outside and buried in the ground. A gravestone marks the site of a grave.

HEALING THE SICK

A Hmong shaman (*right*) is called *txiv neeb*, which means "person of a healing spirit." Shamans beat gongs and shake rattles to heal people who are sick. To remove the dab that has caused the sickness, the shaman drapes a cloth over his head so that he cannot see. He then chants and goes into a dreamlike trance. A shaman might also try to remove an illness by massage or acupuncture, an ancient Chinese practice of inserting needles at certain points on the body to cure sickness. He might also use herbs as medicine. If a part of the patient's body hurts, the shaman might rub a coin on the spot until the skin turns red and the bad spirit escapes.

HMONG CELEBRATIONS

The most important celebration in Vietnam is Tet, or New Year, celebrated between November and December. The Hmong also celebrate Tet. It is a time to call home the souls of dead ancestors, to ask for the help of household spirits, and to banish harmful spirits. Tet is also a time to sing, dance, and dress in new clothes.

New Year Games

During Tet, boys and girls see potential marriage partners in a special game of catch. In this game, boys and girls form lines and throw a ball back and forth to each other. *Lato*, similar to tennis, is another popular New Year game, played with a bamboo ball. Instead of a racket, people use their hands and feet to hit the ball over a net.

Left: A young Blue Hmong girl plays catch during the Hmong New Year in Thailand.

Hmong New Year in Thailand and Laos

The Hmong of northern Thailand and Laos also celebrate New Year, which they call Peb Caug. People perform many rituals over the three-day celebration, mostly to please the main spirit of the house. The male head of household usually performs these rituals.

Above: Special food for Hmong New Year in Laos

Other Celebrations

Harvest time in autumn is another festival time for the Hmong. Marriages are common at this time because families have sold the year's crops and have money to spend on the festivities. At such special times, the Hmong usually hang tree branches over the gates to a village or over the door of a house where a ceremony will take place. The branches are a sign of welcome.

Below: A Hmong man spins a top during Hmong New Year celebrations in Thailand.

HMONG FESTIVALS IN THE UNITED STATES

The Hmong celebrate their festivals wherever they settle. In the United States, St. Paul, Minnesota, and Fresno, California, hold special Hmong festivals. Fresno's New Year festival, held in November or December, is the biggest Hmong festival in the country. It is a great time to see costumes, hear Hmong music, watch traditional dancing, listen to the Hmong language, eat Hmong food, and purchase Hmong stitchery. Special Fourth of July festivities in St. Paul draw more than 25,000 Hmong for a weekend celebration and tournaments.

45

GLOSSARY

acupuncture: a Chinese practice that involves inserting needles into the body to treat sickness or pain

altitude: distance above the surface of the earth

batik: a method for printing designs on fabric using wax and dyes

communism: a political system in which goods are owned in common and given equally to all people

corvée: unpaid labor on government projects

dab (DAH): a spirit

extended family: a group of relatives, including grandparents, aunts and uncles, and cousins

gó lung jià (GOH lwah-DYAH): a two-stringed Hmong violin

hu plig (hoo PLEE): a naming ceremony

kwv txhiaj (goo TEE-yay): Hmong love poetry that is sung

lato (lah-TOH): a Hmong New Year ball game

lineage: descent from a common ancestor

missionary: a person who works to convert others to his or her religion

monsoon: a season characterized by very heavy rainfall

nong rua (nahng TWAH): a Hmong man responsible for spiritual matters

paj ntaub (pahn DAH-OH): Hmong stitchery

polygamy: the practice of marrying more than one person

puae (PYOO-ay): a Hmong trumpet

qeej (KAYN): a wind instrument

refugee: a person who flees to a foreign country to escape danger or oppression at home

shaman: a medicine man or priest who performs healing ceremonies

slash-and-burn agriculture: the practice of cutting and burning trees to clear land for farming

terrace: a ridge cut into a mountainside to create flat land for farming

thatched: covered with a thick mat of straw or another plant material

tonal language: a language in which changing the tone, or pitch, of a word changes its meaning

txiv neeb (zee NANG): a Hmong shaman

FINDING OUT MORE

Books

Beyer, Elmira K. *My Lee Comes to America*. Toronto: Royal Fireworks Press, 1997.

Coburn, Jewell Reinhart. *Jouanah: A Hmong Cinderella*. Arcadia, CA: Shen's Books, 1996.

Livo, Norma J., and Dia Cha. *Folk Stories of the Hmong: Peoples of Laos, Thailand, and Vietnam*. Englewood, CA: Libraries Unlimited, 1991.

Murphy, Nora. *A Hmong Family*. Minneapolis, MN: Lerner Publications Company, 1997.

Shea, Peggy Deitz. *The Whispering Cloth*. Honesdale, PA: Boyds Mill Press, 1995.

Xiong, Ia, and Run-Lin Gou. *The Gift: The Hmong New Year*. El Monte, CA: Pacific Asia Press, 1996.

Videos

Hmong Cultural Presentation. Hmong Cultural Center, 1998.

Journey from Pha Dong. A Decision in the Hills. Hmong ABC Productions, 1998.

The Mississippi: River of Song, Part 1. Acorn Media and the Smithsonian Institution, 1999.

Websites

<http://cvip.fresno.com/~fc039>

<http://www.hmong.org>

<http://www.hmongcenter.org>

<http://www.lib.uci.edu/rrsc/hmong>

<http://ww2.saturn.stpaul.k12.mn.us/hmong/sathmong.html>

Organizations

Hmong American Women's Association
4871 East Kings Canyon Road
Fresno, CA 93727
Tel: (209) 251-9566

Hmong Cultural Center of Minnesota
995 University Avenue West, Suite 214
Saint Paul, MN 55104-4796
Tel: (651) 917-9937
Fax: (651) 917-9978

Hmong National Development, Inc.
1326 18th Street, NW, Suite 200A
Washington, DC 20036
Tel: (202) 463-2118
Fax: (202) 463-2119

INDEX

ABOUT THE AUTHOR

Sandra Millett writes her own column, "Needle 'n Pen," for the *Fort Worth Star Telegram*. She is an author, lecturer, teacher, and quilt judge. She would like to thank the following people who helped with the book: Dr. Lue Vang and Mr. Wangyee Vang; Dr. Norma Livo, Professor of Education, University of Colorado; Dr. Lawrence R. Heaney of the Field Museum, Chicago, Illinois; Chi Kue of the Hmong American Women's Association and Spencer Vue of the Hmong/Lao Media; Carrie Millett; Yeng Vang; Dr. Robert Cooper; and Stephen Gregory of the UNEP World Conservation Monitoring Centre, Cambridge, England.